A Great Mystery—Exploration of Dinosaurs Extinction

Contents

I. Introduction

II. Speculative Theories on Dinosaurs Extinction

III. Most Authoritative and Popular Speculative Theory on Dinosaurs Extinction

IV. Most Possible and Reasonable Cause of Dinosaurs Extinction

V. Conclusion and Revelation

I. Introduction

In the Mesozoic Era more than 200 million years ago, the reptiles are the leading animals on the Earth, So, the Mesozoic Era is also called "Reptiles Era". In the long period of time, they evolved into the reptiles of different kinds. Some of them evolved into the fishes, crocodiles and lizards today. The Dinosaurs are the largest reptile in the Mesozoic Era. They are the huge terrestrial animals living during the period about 240 to 65 million years ago and they can be classified as the vertebrate with great diversity in the Mesozoic Era (about 250—65 million years B.P.). Most of them are terrestrial reptile and a few of them can walk upright.

The Dinosaurs are the most successful and the largest terrestrial reptiles in the Mesozoic Era and have rich varieties in body size, shape and way of life. They are very suitable to live in the marshland and shallow lakes. In the Mesozoic Era, the air is warm and humid, the plants are exuberant, the food is widely available to the Dinosaurs, and they ruled the Earth for more than 100 million years, till somehow they suddenly vanished on the Earth more than 65 million years ago. Only the widespread skeletons, fossils and vestiges of the Dinosaurs are left and discovered.

The Dinosaurs Flourishing in the Mesozoic Era and
Vanishing Suddenly 65 Million Years Ago

With regard to the origin of the Dinosaurs, there is a theory like this: a meteorite containing radioactive elements impacted the Earth, the radioactive elements spread. As a result, the lizards became large in body and turned into the Dinosaurs. If the four legs of a lizard are rectified to stand up, it can be seen that the lizard is a mini Dinosaur.

The history of discovering the Dinosaur fossils can be dated back to long time ago. Before discovering the Iguanodon fossils, the Europeans have known there are many grotesque huge skeletal fossils buried under the ground. However, people at that time did not know what the category of these skeletal fossils is and regarded them as "Remains of Giants". The Chinese collected these unearthed large ancient animal fossils and used them medicine more than 2000 years ago, and call them as "Dragon Bones".

After the Iguanodon fossils are discovered, the scientists compare them with the lizard and conclude that they are the reptiles that are similar to the lizard and have died out long ago.

In 1842, the British paleobiologist Richard Owen (1804--1892) gave them a name for these reptiles in Latin, namely Dinosaur. The name in Latin comprises two word roots, the meaning of the first word root "Dino" is "horrible or frightening", and the meaning of the second word root "Saur" is "lizard". Since then, the Dinosaur ("Horrible Lizard") is the collective name for these reptiles. However, the Dinosaurs are not lizards, they are the first group of senior living creatures capable of walking upright on the Earth.

The Dinosaurs dominated the terrestrial ecosystem of the Earth for more than 160 million years and suddenly disappeared 65 million years ago, it is a great mystery in the history of life evolution on the Earth. The living things or species that disappeared on the Earth are recorded in the fossils. In the Mesozoic stratum, a lot of Dinosaur fossils are discovered, but in the adjacent Cenozoic stratum, no non-avian Dinosaurs fossils are discovered at all, it can be concluded that the Non-avian Dinosaurs become extinct in the Mesozoic Era. Only the avian survived, most scientists recognize the conclusion that "avian is the descendant of the Dinosaur".

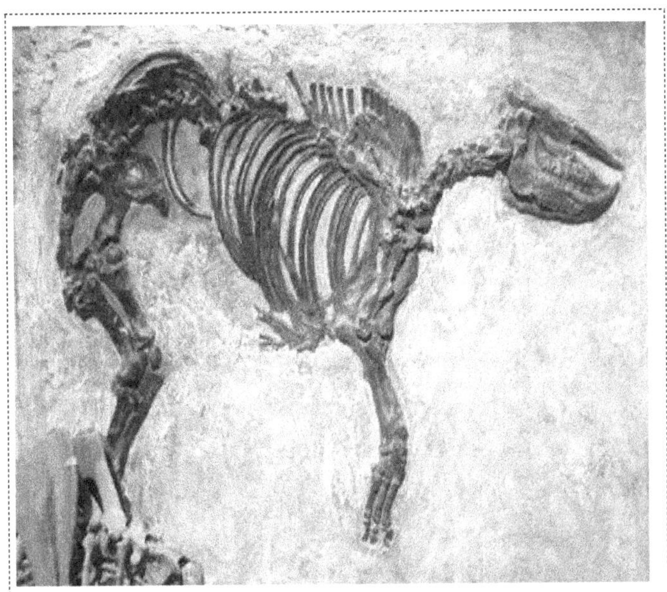

Dinosaur Fossils

"The Origin of Species" (Full Name: *On the Origin of Species by Means of Natural Selection, or the Preservation of Favoured Races in the Struggle for Life*) written by

Charles Darwin (British naturalist, 1809--1882) expounds the emergence of the species, but does not elaborate the disappearance of the species. In the opinions of Darwin, the emergence and disappearance of species are the outcomes of natural evolution. When there is change in natural environment, the species is no longer able to adapt to new environment and there are no other proper place for migration, the quantity of the species will diminish till the species become extinct. Darwin believes that the disappearance of species, same as the emergence of the species, is the effect after slow accumulation of natural selection.

The species on the Earth experienced five mass extinctions, each mass extinction destroyed more than half of the species on the Earth. The Dinosaurs Era came to an end in the fifth mass extinction.

The First Mass Extinction, also called "Ordovician Mass Extinction", started at the end of the Ordovician 440 million years BC, leading to the extinction of about 85% of the species on the Earth.

The Second Mass Extinction, also called "Devonian Mass Extinction", started in the late Devonian Period 365 million years BC, and exterminated the marine life.

The Third Mass Extinction, also called "Permian Mass Extinction", started at the end of Permian Period 250 million years BC, leading to the extinction of more than 96% of species on the Earth.

The Fourth Mass Extinction, also called "Triassic Mass Extinction", started in late Triassic Period 200 million years BC, inflicting heavy losses on the reptiles.

The Fifth Mass Extinction, also called "Cretaceous Mass Extinction" or "Dinosaurs Extinction", started at the end of

Cretaceous Period 65 million years BC, causing the extinction of the Dinosaurs dominating the Earth since Jurassic Period.

II. Speculative Theories on Dinosaurs Extinction

The Dinosaurs became extinct in The Cretaceous–Paleogene (K–Pg) extinction event 65 million years ago. The mystery of the extinction of the Dinosaurs that dominated the terrestrial ecosystem of the Earth for more than 160 million years has been the focus of the research and debate in the science community since the discovery of the Dinosaur fossils. The scientists put forward various speculative theories on the Dinosaurs extinction on the basis of the Dinosaur fossils, totaling more than 130 in number, in an attempt to identify how and why the Dinosaurs became extinct, but all of them are controversial, about 90 of these theories have scientific basis more or less. All these theories are hypotheses rather than conclusive. They have more or less doubts, imperfections and loopholes, or lack adequate evidences, and are challenged by many people. By so far, there is no final conclusion as to the Dinosaurs extinction. The true causes leading to the extinction of the Dinosaurs are still under exploration and debate. The relatively famous theories on the extinction of the Dinosaurs can be summarized as follows:

01. Climate Change Theory.   About 65 million years ago, the Earth climate experienced the great changes, the temperature dropped significantly, causing the fall of oxygen content in the air, the Dinosaurs cannot adapt to such environment with less oxygen and died out. Another **scenario** of the theory is: the Dinosaurs are the Dinosaur is a cold-blooded animal and it has no furs or heat preservation organs and could not survive the low temperature. So, the Dinosaur died of cold. The third scenario of the theory is: the Earth climate changed gradually over a long period, the Dinosaurs could not adapt to the cooler and drier climate and became extinct;

02. Continental Drift Theory.   The geological research proves that there was only one continent on the Earth in the era of Dinosaur, namely the "Pangaea". Due to the change of the Earth crust, the "Pangaea" separated and drifted in the Jurassic Period, leading to the change of environment and climate, therefore, the Dinosaur died out;

03. Geomagnetic Change Theory.   The modern biology proves that the death of some creatures is associated with magnetic field. The creatures sensitive to the magnetic field will die out when there is change in the magnetic field. Hereby the scientists conclude that the extinction of dinosaur is probably associated with the change of magnetic field;

04. Geomagnetism Movement Theory.   In the past eras, the polar circle of geomagnetism moved repeatedly. Each geomagnetism movement triggered the catastrophe leading to the dramatic changes of natural environment, such as flood, tsunami and species extinction, etc., and even the total destruction of civilization. It is natural and inevitable that the Dinosaurs with large body cannot survive such catastrophe;

05. Acid Rain Theory.   The scientists believe that the strong acid rain may fall on the Earth in the end of Cretaceous Period, the microelements in the soil, including strontium, were dissolved. The Dinosaurs directly or indirectly took the strontium through drinking and food, they died out gradually in the end due to chronic poisoning or acute poisoning;

06. Species Struggle Theory.   In the end of Dinosaurs era, the initial small mammalians emerged. They are the rodent predators and probably take Dinosaur eggs as food. As there was no natural enemy for such small animals in the Dinosaur era, they were reproduced more and more in number and ate up the Dinosaur eggs, leading to the extinction of Dinosaur in the end. Another scenario of the theory is: in the Mesozoic Era, the birds and mammals emerged and developed, they are the homeothermal animals capable of adapting to the environmental changes. Compared with the Dinosaurs that are bulky in body, slow in action and stupid in reaction (the head of Dinosaurs is very small relative to their huge body, so the brain is quite limited), the birds and mammals are swift and clever in the fight for food, they are the natural winners. Gradually, the Dinosaurs perished on the Earth due to the failure to get food;

07. Angiosperms Poisoning Theory.   In the end of Dinosaurs Era, namely the Cretaceous Period, the gymnosperm on the Earth died out and was replaced by massive angiosperm that contains the toxic alkaloid. As the Dinosaurs are huge in body and food intake is extra big, the over accumulation of the toxin of angiosperm in the body poisoned the Dinosaurs in the end;

08. Volcano Activity Theory. When the undersea and land volcano erupts, the massive carbon dioxide is spouted, causing the acute greenhouse effect on the Earth and leading to the death of the plants. Furthermore, the halogen is released in massive scale along with volcano eruption, the ozone layer breaks up, the harmful ultraviolet light shines over the surface of the Earth, causing the death of species. Another scenario of the theory is: the volcano activity significantly decreases the Sun's radiation, the volcanic eruption throws the dust into the air and the dust turns into suspended solids in the air, the acid rain forms. They are the primary contributors to the extinction of species on the Earth;

09. Orogenesis Theory. The Orogenesis occurring at the end of Cretaceous Period dried out the swamplands, the Dinosaurs dependent on the swamplands no longer can survive. Due to the climate change, the plants were changed, the herbivorous Dinosaurs cannot adapt to the new plants and died out gradually, the predatory Dinosaurs dependent on the herbivorous Dinosaurs also died out consequently. The extinction process of Dinosaurs lasted 10~20 million years. By the end of Cretaceous Period, the Dinosaurs perished totally on the Earth;

10. Sudden Temperature Drop Theory. Dinosaurs are warm-blooded animals, they have relative high metabolism rate and can maintain a fixed temperature. However, the respiratory organs of the Dinosaurs are imperfect and they cannot supply the adequate oxygen to the respiratory organs. So, the body temperature of Dinosaurs is not high and may be close to the modern bradypod. To maintain such body temperature, the Dinosaurs can only live in the tropical zone. If the body temperature of Dinosaurs drops to a specific level, the physical fitness has to be consumed to raise the body temperature, otherwise, the heat must be preserved. As the body of Dinosaurs is too huge to shelter themselves in the caves, the Dinosaurs will die of cold due to exhaustion of physical fitness if the cold days last a long time;

11. Cannibalism Theory. Due to the climate change, the plants died out, the herbivorous Dinosaurs became extinct gradually, the predatory Dinosaurs became crazy due to the lack of food, they killed each other and died out in the end;

12. Oppression Theory. The number of Dinosaurs increased dramatically, the limited plants cannot support the existence of the herbivorous Dinosaurs, leading to the extinction of them, then the predatory Dinosaurs died out due to the shortage of food;

13. Temperature Deciding Sex Theory. Pursuant to the condition of crocodile, the sex of crocodile is decided by the air temperature of egg stage. When the temperature is high, the crocodile in the egg is male; when the temperature is low, the crocodile in the egg is female. As the crocodile remains the primitive of the Dinosaurs, the sex of Dinosaur egg may be similar to the crocodile in this respect. Due to the sudden change of the Earth climate and the upsurge of temperature 65 million years ago, almost all the Dinosaur eggs became male, leading to no reproduction and final extinction of Dinosaurs;

14. Sudden Climate Change Theory. Based on the data obtained from deep-sea geological drilling, some scientists conclude that the Earth climate 65 million years ago experienced abnormal changes and the temperature rose suddenly. The poikilothermal animals weak in heat dissipation, including the Dinosaurs, cannot adapt to such changes, which gives rise to the endocrine system disorder and causes serious damage to the reproductive system of male Dinosaurs. As a result, the Dinosaurs cannot reproduce offsprings and become extinct in the end;

There is another scenario of the theory, it agrees that the sudden climate change leads to the extinction of the Dinosaurs, but has different speculation: about 70 million years ago, the Arctic Ocean is totally separated by the continents with other oceans, and in the last days, the salty seawater gradually becomes fresh water under the actions of various factors. About 65 million years ago, the "Embankment" separating the Arctic Ocean and other oceans suddenly breached, much seawater of the Arctic Ocean, which is lighter due to desalination, flows into other oceans. As the temperature of the seawater of the Arctic Ocean is very low, the cold water overflowing from the Arctic Ocean formed a cold ocean current, the seawater temperature of the oceans dropped by appropriately $20\,^{\circ}\mathrm{C}$. The fall of ocean temperature produces severe effect on the continental climate, the air on the continents is cooled sharply, water vapor content and oxygen content in the air decrease dramatically and the continents become arid. The sudden climate change leads to the extinction of the Dinosaurs;

15. Species Aging Theory. As the boom period of the Dinosaurs lasts 160 million years, the body of them became too huge, the horns and other skeletons over developed in such long-period evolution, which caused great inconveniences in living and looking for food and led to the extinction in the end. Apatosaurus, a most representative Dinosaur, is 25 meters long and weighs 30 metric tons. As the body is too large, Apatosaurus is very slow in action and lost the viability. Besides, due to the continuous growth of three horns and over development of skeleton protecting the head, Triceratops became extinct in the end;

16. Sea Level Receding Theory.   When sea level recedes, the lands are connected. The creatures contact or affect each other, causing the extinction of some creatures. For instance, kangaroos can only live in the Australian Continent, and they will be eaten off by other animals if they live on the South American Continent. In addition to such eating and being eaten relationship (food chain model), the infection and propagation of diseases and parasites are likely to cause the extinction of Dinosaurs; another scenario of the theory is: the sea level recedes notably 65 million years ago, causing the change of the Earth temperature, the original natural conditions for the reproduction of the Dinosaurs no longer exists. So, the Dinosaurs gradually died out;

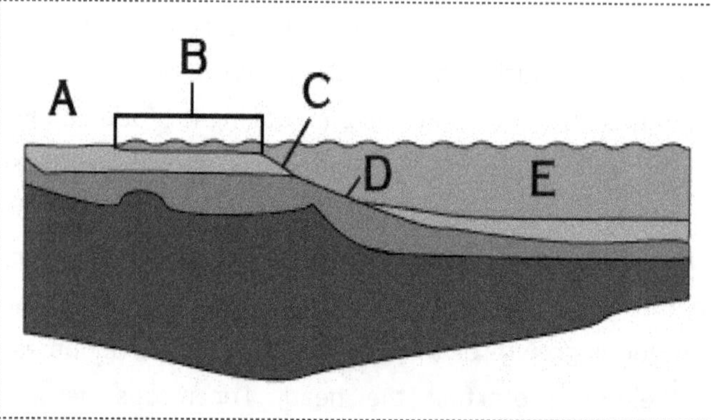

Massive Sea Level Receding

A- Coast,   B- Continental Shelf,   C- Continental Slope,   D- Continental Base,   E-Ocean

17. Universe Particles Flow Storm Theory.   The Earth once fell into a strong universe particles flow storm. The particles intruding the Earth at a high speed "tear" the molecule into the condensation nucleus necessary for the formation of rain, finally leading to the more thick cloud layer, more frequent rainfall and sharp temperature drop. The scientists believe that it is the outbreak of universe particles flow that causes the drastic changes of the Earth climate conditions. As the Dinosaurs cannot adapt to such climate changes, they became extinct in a short period;

18. Atmospheric Constituents Change Theory.   The modern scientific analysis indicates that there is little oxygen and high content of carbon dioxide in the air in the remote years when the Earth takes its initial form. Later, autotrophic organisms emerged, the photosynthesis started the process of consuming the carbon dioxide and making oxygen, thus changing the atmosphere environment on the Earth. Meanwhile, the carbon dioxide

A Great Mystery—Exploration of Dinosaurs Extinction

deposits in the stratum in the forms of coal and fossil oil through biological fixation, and also deposits in the forms of various carbonate through organic or inorganic process. Such deposits are going on all the time. The evidences show that the density of carbon dioxide is very high in the Mesozoic Era during which the Dinosaurs lived, while in the subsequent Cenozoic Era, the density of carbon dioxide is quite low. It is well known that each species needs a proper environment for normal growth. The primary elements of environment include air, water, temperature and ecosystem, etc. The environmental changes directly affect or decide the fate of a species. The high content of carbon dioxide in the air in the Mesozoic Era when the Dinosaurs lived indicates that the Dinosaurs well adapt to the atmospheric environment with high density of carbon dioxide, only in such atmospheric environment, can they well live. At the end of Cretaceous Period, great changes took place in the atmospheric environment, the content of carbon dioxide decreased and the content of oxygen increased. The new atmospheric environment is not favorable to the Dinosaurs. It made the Dinosaurs vulnerable to various diseases that can propagate like pandemic. On the other hand, the new atmospheric environment is more suitable to the survival and growth of mammals and the mammals become the new advanced and more adaptable competitor on the Earth. Under the action of these two factors, the Dinosaurs become extinct in the end;

The theory is based on two points: first, the atmospheric constituents in the Mesozoic Era are different from the same in the modern times, which can be proved by modern science; second, each species needs a suitable atmospheric environment for survival. The atmosphere in the Paleozoic Era contains little oxygen and has a very high content of carbon dioxide. With the emergence of organisms, the content of carbon dioxide decreased gradually and the content of oxygen increased gradually in the air under the action of photosynthesis. This process can explain many questions in the history of life evolution on the Earth. For instance, the Life Explosion in the Cambrian Period is a puzzle in the history of life evolution. The Atmospheric Constituents Change Theory may be the proper answer to this puzzle, the argument for which is: as animal cannot directly use inorganics to make photosynthesis, its origin is naturally later than the origin of plant, and will not start until the oxygen content in the air reaches a specific level. So, the Life Explosion in the in the Cambrian Period must be subject to the condition that the oxygen content reaches a level necessary for triggering the origin of life, which has been proven by the modern science;

19. Meteoroids Impacting the Earth Theory.   The recent findings indicate that the massive meteoroid impacting may be the primary contributor to the extinction of Dinosaurs. At the end of Cretaceous Period 65 million years ago, meteoroids impacted the Earth, thus killing all the Dinosaurs overnight. The immediate evidence for the theory is that there is no Dinosaur fossil during the period of 3 million years;

20. Species Decline Theory.   The total decline of survival system and life mechanism of the Dinosaurs is the root cause of the Dinosaur's extinction. Any species has the specific life cycle on the Earth. When the life recycle comes to an end, any species will die out automatically. The facts proved that the Dinosaurs declined prior to the arrival of so-called "Great Catastrophe";

21. Sexual Performance Decline Theory. Affected by the geologic climate and geological factors, the male Dinosaurs encountered sexual dysfunction in the end of Cretaceous Period, a large number of Dinosaur eggs cannot be fertilized, leading to the extinction of the Dinosaurs. From the early period to the late period of Cretaceous Period, the Dinosaur eggs fossils in the stratum decreased gradually, the number of Dinosaurs reduced continuously, coming to the extinction in the end;

22. Farting Extinguishing the Dinosaurs Theory. Most of the Dinosaurs are huge in body and numerous in quantity, some of them weigh 80 to 100 tons and eat 130~260 kilograms of food a day, they keep on farting. As the fart contains much methane gas, the accumulated methane gas in the air destroyed the ozone layer, leading to the disastrous change of Earth ecology, devastating climate and terrible food shortage, the Dinosaurs became extinct in the end;

23. Organosilicon Deficiency Theory. The muscle of the Dinosaurs is a silicone. The silicone content in the body of the Dinosaurs is higher than that of animals' ancestors. The Dinosaurs are highly dependent on the silicon hydride. The Dinosaurs take the animals and plants of with macromolecule organic silicon or silicone structure as the food. With the decrease of such food, the Dinosaurs died out gradually;

24. Pandemic Extinguishing the Dinosaurs Theory. When the Sunspot activity reaches peak, the Sun will emit abundant high energy particles and X-ray, triggering the geomagnetic storms and causing the climatic anomaly, the microorganisms propagates massively on the Earth, the pandemic breaks out, the Dinosaurs die out;

25. Comet Impacting the Earth plus Volcano Activity Theory. The hard evidences found by the scientists prove that a huge comet impacted the Earth 65 million years ago, causing the volcano eruption. With the volcano eruption, the massive anaerobic bacteria are released. The anaerobic bacteria convert the oxygen into a poisonous chemical gas, the oxygen in the air becomes scarce gradually. The Dinosaurs with huge body no longer can survive and become extinct in the end;

26. Massive Undersea Volcanic Activity Theory. At the end of Cretaceous Period, a series of massive undersea volcanic eruptions broke out, thereby affecting the heat balance of seawater and triggering the change of terrestrial climate, the living environment of the Dinosaurs is changed. As the Dinosaurs cannot adapt to the new environment, they died out gradually;

27. Regular Mass Extinction Event Theory. Some scientists believe that the Solar System moves past the two wings of Milky Way Galaxy every 200—500 million years. When the Solar System moves past the two wings of the Milky Way Galaxy, the atmosphere will be polluted by hydrogen, causing the mass extinction, the Dinosaurs perished consequently;

28. Supernova Explosion Theory. About 65 million years ago, a supernova exploded, massive heavy elements were thrown out in the explosion, the heavy elements fell down to the Earth and strong cosmic rays radiated the Earth, leading to the extinction of the Dinosaurs. Another **scenario** of the theory is: a supernova nearby the Earth exploded, the massive meteoric shower impacted the

Earth, large dusts and poisonous gases flood the atmosphere of the Earth, the large animals, particularly the Dinosaurs, are killed off. The evidences are: the Moon may be the outcome of such impacting; the poisonous gases can make gene mutation, particularly for the cells with great activity, including the sperm and ovum;

29. Crust Movement Theory. At the end of the Mesozoic Era, owing to the crust movement, the Earth temperature dropped dramatically, the ice covered the land. As Dinosaurs are cold-blooded animals, they cannot withstand the cold environment and gradually died out. Another **scenario** of the theory is: cold-blooded animals are more dependent on the sunlight temperature than the warm-blooded animals. Temperature is vital to the animals and plants, the Dinosaurs are huge in body and have no furs to preserve the heat. As the Dinosaurs could not adapt to the environmental temperature changes, they are eliminated by the nature. The birds, small cold-blooded reptiles, panda, crocodiles, whales, mice, inspects and other animals living in the same era of the Dinosaurs survived as they are small in body, consume less energy and have furs to preserve the body temperature;

30. Over Successful Evolution Theory. As the Dinosaurs are the most advanced animals in evolution in the Mesozoic Era, they are the top rulers of the Earth in the Era and have no natural enemies. So, they are too suitable to and too heavily dependent on the environment. When the catastrophe or outside forces changes the climate and living environment, it is very hard for the Dinosaurs to adapt to new environment and survive, just as an enterprise with too heavy dependence on one single client or a few clients is fragile and cannot survive the fierce market competition. When the evolution of a species comes to an end, the survival of the species will become very fragile;

31. Comet Impacting the Earth Theory.   About 65 million years ago, a comet impacted the Earth, triggering the explosion and burning, the oxygen in the air is consumed up, suffocating the Dinosaurs. The evidence for the theory is that some elements do not exist on the Earth.   Another **scenario** of the theory is: in the Mesozoic Era, the comet impacted the Earth, causing the great change of the Earth surface.   The Dinosaurs cannot adapt to the new environment and perished. The third scenario of the theory is: the gravity of Nemesis, a semi-star of the Sun, pushes the Comet to the Earth periodically, the Comet impacted the Earth, leading to the mass extinction of the species, including the Dinosaurs, and such mass extinction comes every 26 million years;

32. Sudden Change of Environment Theory.   At the end of Cretaceous Period, the volcanic activity is frequently. The volcanic ash not only polluted the air seriously, but also overshadowed the sunlight over the years, thus causing the sudden change of the ecological environment, the oxygen is scarce, no rain falls, the marshes and mountains are dried up and the plants become extinct. In such severe environment, the Dinosaurs died out;

33. Aliens Exterminating the Dinosaurs Theory. According to the theory, the aliens hunted the Dinosaurs 60 million years ago and eliminated the Dinosaurs in several thousand years. In the eyes of the aliens, the Dinosaurs are merely the delicious chickens. They hunted several hundred tons of the Dinosaurs a year. The Dinosaurs graveyard discovered in the Arctic testified the theory. In the Dinosaurs graveyard there, the sharp vestiges left by laser cutting can found on the bones of the Dinosaurs. The evidences show that the aliens once took the Dinosaurs to their planet and reared them as livestock, probably the aliens realize that the Dinosaurs are on the verge of extinction at that time. Some scientists support the theory, arguing that the over hunting on the Earth leads to the extinction of many animals;

34. Constipation Theory. The cycas and bracken are the primary food of the herbivorous Dinosaurs. Later, the cycas and bracken became extinct, the Dinosaurs turned to eat the mulberries, causing the constipation, and died out due to the indigestion;

35. Oviparity Causing Dinosaurs Extinction Theory. A female Dinosaur weighs 4 metric tons, 2500 times heavier than her new baby, while the weight of a female elephant is only 22 times the weight of her baby. In other words, the baby of mammals is much bigger than the baby of Dinosaurs, reason for which is: for the Dinosaurs, to procreate a baby with quite big body, the eggshell must be more big and thick and the embryo can breathe through eggshell structure, it is impossible to meet such requirements. So, the baby Dinosaurs are sure to be eliminated by the mammals in the survival competition, the Dinosaurs become extinct in the end;

36. Diseases Killing Off Dinosaurs Theory. The Theory believes that a mysterious virus similar to the AIDS today or a pandemic suddenly swept across the Earth during the peak prosperity period of the Dinosaurs, killing off the Dinosaurs dominating the Earth for 140 million years;

37. Reproduction Failure Theory. The cooling of the Earth generated severe impact on the eggs of the

Dinosaurs. Some scientists find out that the shell of the Dinosaur eggs became thinner at the end of Cretaceous Period, and the Dinosaur eggs at the end of Cretaceous Period have less pores than the same in other periods of Mesozoic Era, these findings indicate that the reproduction of the Dinosaurs failed due to the cooling of the Earth climate, the Dinosaurs perished on the Earth in the end; another scenario of the theory is: owing to the climate cooling resulting from the natural change of Earth climate, the Dinosaur eggs cannot be incubated into baby Dinosaurs, leading to the extinction of the Dinosaurs;

38. Gender Imbalance Theory.   Owing to cold climate, the most of Dinosaur babies incubated by the female Dinosaurs are female ones, causing the severe gender imbalance in the Dinosaurs family. With the diminishing of female Dinosaurs, the Dinosaurs perished on the Earth;

39. Ice Age Theory.   Throughout the history of the Earth, the ice age is a regular climate. In the ice age, the temperature drops dramatically and the water is frozen. The scientists discovered that the fossils of some Dinosaurs are frozen in the huge ice rock, and speculate that a global cold transformation once happened in the Dinosaurs era, the mountains and rivers are covered with snow and ice, the Dinosaurs cannot withstand the cold and find the food, they are not able to live under such harsh conditions, they perished on the Earth in the end;

40. Volcanic Activity and Earthquake Theory.   At the end of Cretaceous Period, the volcanic activity and earthquake are frequent, the natural environment suitable to the survival of the Dinosaurs is destroyed, the Dinosaurs died out;

41. Excessive Reproduction Theory.   The reproduction of

A Great Mystery—Exploration of Dinosaurs Extinction

the Dinosaurs is excessive, the speed of oxygen production on the Earth cannot catch up with the speed of Dinosaurs reproduction, the Dinosaurs perished due to the scarce oxygen;

42. Warm-Blooded Animal Theory. The Dinosaurs are warm-blooded animals, so, they cannot withstand and survive the cold climate in the late Cretaceous Period. The reasons are: the body temperature of the Dinosaurs is still low although they are warm-blooded animals, and may be close to the temperature of the modern sloths. To maintain such body temperature, the Dinosaurs can only live in the tropical zone. Besides, the respiratory organs of the Dinosaurs are imperfect, they cannot supply the adequate oxygen to the body of the Dinosaurs. The Dinosaurs have no thick fur to preserve the heat, furthermore, their long tail and feet consume much heat. The difference that distinguishing the warm-blooded animals and cold-blooded animals is: when the body temperature of warm-blooded animals drops below a specific level, they must consume the physical strength to preserve the body temperature and their body will become very weak. Moreover, the body of the Dinosaurs is too big to shelter themselves in the caves. So, if the cold days last a long period, the Dinosaurs will die of cold after exhausting the physical strength;

43. Aerolite Impacting the Earth Theory. Some scientists speculate that an aerolite from outer space crashed into the ocean of the Earth at the speed of 40km per second about 65 million years ago, 4 seconds later, a deep crafter came out, the steam column of hot seawater rose up to 40km, the sea waves five kilometers high and the gasified aerolite dust engulfed the Earth. Soon, the snow on the polar was melted, the plants were destroyed and the Dinosaurs were buried under the ground, the Dinosaurs became extinct. Naturally, the aerolite is also likely to crash on a continent and it will bring about more severe extinction to the species on the Earth;

Another scenario of the theory is: a very huge aerolite impacted the Earth 65 million years ago, causing the sudden rise of the Earth water temperature to a very high level, meanwhile, the aerolite brought about the massive radioactive elements to the Earth, under the co-action of these two factors, the Dinosaurs became extinct;

The third scenario of the theory is: Based on the study on the Iridium on the Earth, scientists believe that an aerolite with a diameter of 10km impacted the Earth violently at the speed of 25km per hour 65 million years ago, it produced a big explosion equal to the explosion of 100 trillion tons of explosives and threw massive dust into the atmosphere. The dust blocked the sunlight for 3 months and the Earth fell into darkness. The plants died, the Dinosaurs had no food to eat and starved to death;

The fourth scenario of the theory is: An aerolite impacted the Earth 65 million years ago, the Earth experienced long darkness. Owing to no sunlight, the climate changed and the Earth cooled, the plants died due to the lack of sunlight and appropriate climate. The Dinosaurs with huge body and voracious appetite died out gradually due to the food shortage, the Dinosaur eggs could not be incubated into baby Dinosaurs because of no sunlight and enough temperature. The Dinosaurs are eliminated on the Earth in the end;

44. Extreme Evolution Theory. The Dinosaurs, as the hegemon of the Earth in the Mesozoic Era, dominated the

A Great Mystery—Exploration of Dinosaurs Extinction

terrestrial ecosystem for 160 million years, they are at the top of the animals and have no natural enemies in that Era. It is no doubt that they are the species that have evolved to the top limit. However, such extreme evolution is achieved at the expense of other aptitudes. In the species evolution, two kinds of species, namely the species at the top and the species at the bottom, are eliminated first, the species at the middle are preserved. The species with extreme evolution require the extreme environment for survival, while the species at the bottom are naturally squeezed by other species in living space. So, the extreme evolution contributes to the extinction of the Dinosaurs;

45. "Death Star" Theory. The theory believes that a celestial body revolving around the Sun will throw some asteroids to the Sun every 26 million years, a part of the asteroids impact the Earth, leading to the extinction of the Dinosaurs. The "Death Star" is called "Fury", it is the "Chief Culprit" for the extinction of the Dinosaurs;

46. Mercury Incurring Disaster Theory. The theory believes that the extinction of the Dinosaurs could be attributed to the Mercury. The scientists use the computer modeling to "restore" the Solar System 250 million years ago. The modeling indicates that the orbit of the Mercury deviated 65 million years ago and produced impact on an asteroid belt in outer space. It is very likely that a single asteroid collided with the Earth, thus causing the extinction of the Dinosaurs;

47. Crust Movement plus Earth Climate Change Theory. In the early and middle periods of Mesozoic Era 70 million years ago, the Dinosaurs family is flourishing and dominant on the Earth. At that time, the climate is warm, the lakes and marshes are widespread, the animals and plants available for food is very abundant, the Dinosaurs live a rich and stable life. Their body structure is only adaptable to the then natural conditions and such adaptability is fixed in the long period of time. In the late period of Mesozoic Era (Cretaceous Period), a number of mountains grow on the crust, the marshes are destroyed and the Earth climate changed, cold and hot seasons come out alternatively, the air becomes dry and hot. The Dinosaurs, as cold-blooded animals, could not adapt to such changes. Their respiratory organs are only adaptable to the wet and hot air, the Dinosaurs feel very uncomfortable in the dry and hot air. Owing to the Earth climate change, the once-exuberant gymnosperm died out and is replaced by the angiosperm that blossom and yield fruit. When the winter comes, the plants wither. The Dinosaurs face severe food shortage. As the body structure of the Dinosaurs has become fixed and unchangeable in the long evolution, the Dinosaurs have no way out in the new environment. The snakes and lizards that can hibernate, and small mammals and the birds that have cold-proof furs and can shelter themselves in the caves survived the new environment;

48. Eggshell Thickening Theory.   The archaeologists find out that almost all the discovered Dinosaur egg fossils fall within the Cretaceous Period, where do the Dinosaur eggs in the Triassic Period and Jurassic Period go? The only one answer is: they are incubated into the baby Dinosaurs. Another question comes up: why the Dinosaur eggs in late Cretaceous Period could not be incubated into baby Dinosaurs? After careful research, the archaeologists find the answer.   They conclude that the Dinosaur eggshell in late Cretaceous Period thickens under the stimulation by outside environment, the Dinosaur eggs could not be incubated into baby Dinosaurs. So, the Dinosaurs died out;

49. Natural Environment and Climate Theory.   In Triassic Period and Jurassic Period, the Earth climate is very warm and moist and has no obvious change of four seasons, the plants are very exuberant, the tall and large gingkoes, ferns, cycads, pines and cypresses grow everywhere. These plants are the food favored most by the Dinosaurs. The phytophagous Dinosaurs have the food to eat at any time. However, in the Cretaceous Period, the natural environment and climate on the Earth start to change, the climate alternates with four seasons, the two polar regions are cooled, the plants favored most by the phytophagous Dinosaurs could not adapt to the new climate and environment and died out, the phytophagous Dinosaurs starve to death, the number of carnivorous Dinosaurs decreased dramatically. So, the Dinosaurs became extinct in the end;

50. Multiple Causes Coaction Theory (or Butterfly Effect Theory).   The theory believes that the extinction of the Dinosaurs is a very complicated process. One single cause cannot contribute to the extinction of the Dinosaurs. The extinction of the Dinosaurs is the outcome of the coaction of multiple causes. Regardless whatever happened at that time, one thing is certain that the Dinosaurs cannot adapt to or rise to the things that have come up, so they perished mysteriously on the Earth in the end. The scenario of the theory is: In late Cretaceous Period, the crust movement is very active, it changed the original natural environment, the circulation pattern of ocean and atmosphere is broken (for instance, the orogenesis occurring in the end of Cretaceous Period dried the marsh, the Dinosaurs dependent on the marsh no longer could survive). The active crust movement triggered massive volcanic eruptions, the huge volcanic ash, carbon dioxide and poisonous gases are spouted and join the disordered atmosphere circulation, causing the drastic change of climate. Furthermore, the volcanic eruptions discharge the halogen in large scale, the ozone layer is damaged and the harmful ultraviolet rays directly irradiate the Earth surface. So, the situations like these come up concurrently: greenhouse effect, substantial increase of seawater evaporation, sea level receding, poisonous dust covering up the sky, darkness and acid rain, extreme cold and hot climate, massive death of plants and growing severe food shortage. In such harsh environment, the fight between the Dinosaurs for food further intensified, they kill each other or are killed by more advanced mammals, the Dinosaur eggs are eaten up by other animals or could not be incubated, the Dinosaurs became extinct in the end.

The above theories are only relative popular and scientific ones of the theories as to how the Dinosaurs became extinct. A common point of the most of the above-cited theories is that the massive extinction of the Dinosaurs is closely or directly associated with the climate changes caused by various factors, including inside and outside ones. One thing is certain that no theory is absolutely proven or is final and no one exactly knows how and why the Dinosaurs became extinct. Everyone can put forward his own opinion based on his knowledge and imagination.

III. Most Authoritative and Popular Speculative Theory on Dinosaurs Extinction

Among the speculative theories on Dinosaurs extinction, the most authoritative and popular one is the Asteroid Impacting Theory by so far. The Theory believes that the extinction of the Dinosaurs can be attributed to an asteroid impacting the Earth 65 million years ago. Based on the relevant research findings, the scientists describe the spectacular scenario of the event 65 million years ago: One day, the Dinosaurs are enjoying their happy time in their Earth paradise, suddenly, a glaring white light comes out in the sky, an asteroid with a diameter of 10km and a size of a middle-city, crashed into the ocean on the Earth at 40 times the speed of the sound (20km/second), it made a huge and deep crater in the ocean floor and triggered a gigantic explosion. The seawater is vaporized quickly, the steam spurts tens of thousands meters high into the sky, the subsequent tsunami is as high as 5 kilometers and spread at extreme fast speed, the turbulent surge engulfs the surface of the Earth. Meanwhile, the ground trembles violently in the collision, the super earthquake exceeding magnitude 12 breaks out, the cracks come out on the ground, the mountains collapse. A few days later, the shock wave comes together at the other end of the Earth, triggers the violent earthquake, shattering the crust there. The magma deep inside the Earth spurts out after the crust is shattered, triggering the violent volcanic eruption on Deccan Plateau in India, meanwhile, the movement direction of Earth's tectonic plates is changed. The asteroid impacting the Earth is a huge rock as large as a high mountain.

Asteroid Impacting the Earth

The asteroid impacting event 65 million years ago is a horrible and super violent catastrophe and no one event in human history can rival it. The volume of the asteroid is very huge, when the asteroid crashed on the Earth, its tail still stays at the sky 35,000 feet high, equal to the flying altitude of jet airliner. It radiates brilliant light when falling down to the Earth. The big explosion at the impacting place is equal to the explosion of several billions of atomic bombs. The explosion produced massive rocks, flying apart more than 640 kilometers away in all directions and forming the rock windrow 15 meters high. Within this range, all the lives are buried alive in the moment. The impacting also triggers huge shock wave, the shock wave radiate outward, forming the tornado at the speed of 1600km/hour, all the trees and large animals are destroyed. As the impacting place is in the shallow sea, seawater is splashed up, forming the tsunami, the 150-meter high surge rushes to the coast of Gulf of Mexico, devouring all the lives on the land within several kilometers in the moment.

The rocks and dust spouted out of the impact crater fly into the sky, then fall down to the Earth, the dust envelops the Earth. Meanwhile, numberless meteorites intrude into the atmosphere, the horrible sea of fire comes out in the sky, the burning meteorites fall down on the Earth, everything on the Earth seem to be kindled by blaze, the Earth falls into the sea of fire.

About half of the forests are destroyed totally, the blaze in each place discharges 10 trillion tons of carbon dioxide, carbon monoxide and methane gas, the air is severely polluted and is suffocating. The sky rains at last, but the rain is the corrosive acid rain, the ecosystem of the Earth is damaged severely.

The asteroid impacting produced the dust covering the sky and super-high heat, the snow in the polar region is melted, the plants are destroyed, the volcanic ash fills up the sky. The Earth falls into darkness, the temperature drops dramatically, the Earth is cooled, the torrential rain falls, the forests catch fire, torrential flood roars down from the mountains, the tsunami, flood and mud-rock flow carried away and buried the Dinosaurs and other species. In the subsequent days and years, the sky is still occupied by the dust, smoke and black clouds. As no sunlight reaches the Earth for years, the Earth entered into the darkness and Ice Age, leading to the extinction of the Dinosaurs and 75% of species on the Earth, the land becomes silent. It is the end of the world caused by the catastrophe from the universe. The Dinosaurs era in the history of biology comes to an end, it is called Cretaceous–Paleogene (K–Pg) extinction event (K-Pg Event, the 5th Mass Extinction on the Earth).

Asteroid Impacting the Earth and Extinction of the Dinosaurs

The best and direct evidence for the theory is a remote impact crater called Chicxulub Crater discovered by the geologists in 1991 in Yucatan Peninsula, Mexico, the diameter of the crater is about 180km. In the Crater, there is a white rock stratum called K-T Boundary by the geologists, meaning the marking line of Cretaceous-Tertiary boundary. The geologists find that under the K-T Boundary there are rich Dinosaur fossils, and above the K-T boundary, no Dinosaur fossils are discovered. Furthermore, the K-T boundary has rich content of iridium, a rare metal. The average content of such metal on the Earth is only part per billion, while the iridium content in the K-T boundary is 200 times the normal content. Such high content of iridium can only be found in the space. The iridium content in the space is 1000 times higher than that in the Earth. In addition, the shocked quartz is found in the K-T boundary. Only the asteroid can leave such mark. The high content of iridium and shocked quartz are found in the K-T boundary stratum of many places on the Earth. Such global vestiges only stems from the most violent Asteroid impacting. Based on the analysis of the above research findings and by reflecting on the "Squashed Sand", the geologists conclude that a huge asteroid impacted the Earth 65million years ago, the Chicxulub Crater is the place impacted by the asteroid and such super powerful and violent impacting is the primary contributor to the extinction of the Dinosaurs.

The asteroid impacting the Earth is a huge rock with a diameter of 10 kilometers. The diameter of the caldera caused by the impacting is as wide as 200 kilometers. Based on the huge size of the crater, the scientists estimate that the energy produced by the asteroid impacting is 10 billion times the energy of the atomic bomb dropped on Hiroshima, Japan.

The energy produced by the impacting is equal to the energy produced by the explosion of one megaton of dynamite. Through the atmosphere, the dust produced by the big explosion after the asteroid impacting spread to form a cloud layer, covering the Earth and blocking the sunlight, the Earth falls into darkness for several months (at least 3 months, some scientists believe that such horrible darkness last one to two years), During this period, the photosynthesis of the plants is interrupted, the plants withered and died in massive scale, the Dinosaurs died out due to the lack of food.

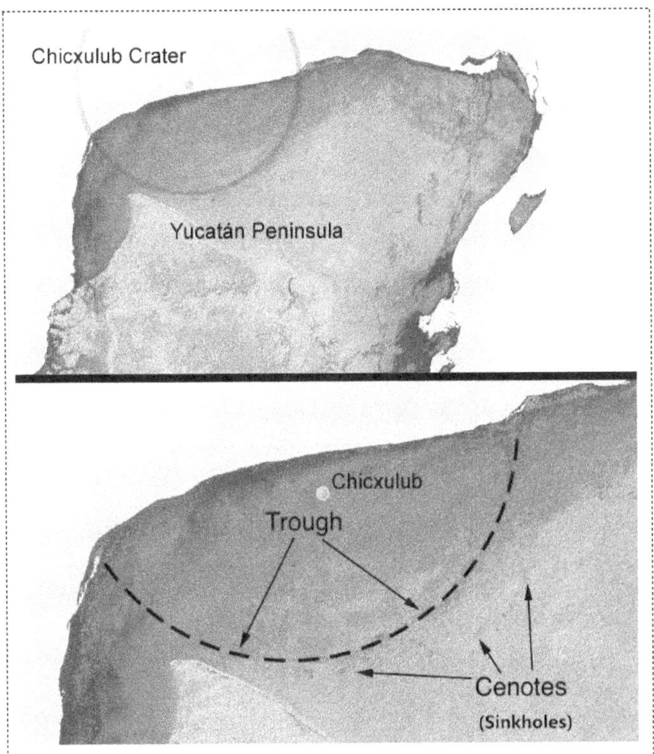

The Chicxulub Crater in Yucatan Peninsula presents an oval, the average diameter is about 180km, and it is the largest impact crater on the surface of the Earth.

As the asteroid impacting place is located in the Yucatan Peninsula, North America is the first to bear the brunt of such huge asteroid impacting. The powerful shock waves produced by the impacting triggered the strong earthquake and large tsunami, engulfing the whole North America. It is the tsunami that devoured large numbers of freshwater fishes, vertebrates, trees, ammonites and shellfishes, and other marine organism in the moment, the remains of them are reserved in the stratum of North America in that way.

The strength of the asteroid impacting the Yucatan Peninsula is huge, amazing and awesome. The scientists detected a 550-meter high ring mountain about 30km underneath the Yucatan Peninsula, it is a peak ring crater formed after the asteroid impacted the Earth and is the only one ring mountain on the Earth, it is the famous Chicxulub Crater. The granites of the ring mountain show the huge strength of the asteroid impacting the Earth. The huge impacting stirred the granites deep inside the Earth to the surface of the Earth, forming a 550-meter high ring mountain and making a peak ring crater with a diameter of 180km.

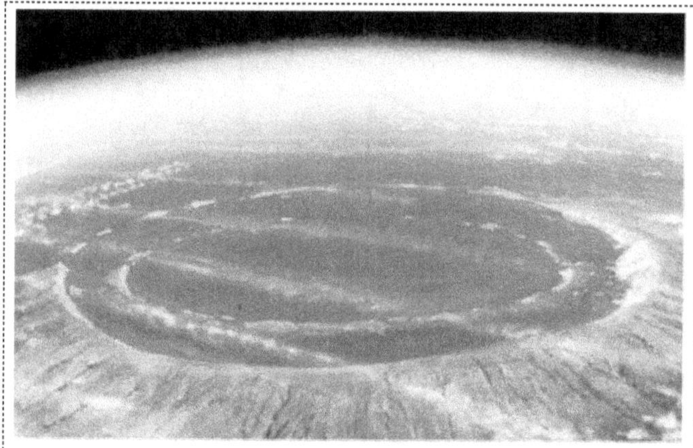

The Huge Chicxulub Crater Formed after the Asteroid Impacting the Earth and Detected by Scientists underneath the Yucatan Peninsula. The height of the ring mountain is 550 meters and the diameter of the crater is 180km.

In April, 2019, a team of archaeologists from University of Kansas discovered a large graveyard buried with the fossils of large numbers of Dinosaurs, fishes and other animals in

North Dakota. The graveyard becomes another key evidence for the asteroid impacting the Earth 65 million years ago.

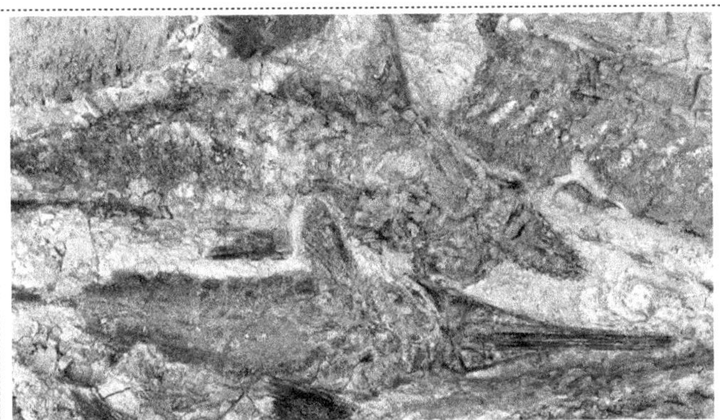

The Fossil Fish Cut into Two Halves---The Fish Collides with Tree and is Broken into Two Halves when Tsunami Comes

All the things are preserved in live form and are not squashed or crushed, reflecting the situation that the strength of tsunami is powerful enough to kill the organisms instantly. The archaeologists find that some fishes obviously inhaled the eruptive materials related to the asteroid impacting before they are killed, and worked out that the age of the materials attached on the fossil fishes is about 65.76 million years, it is consist with the time when the Chicxulub Crater is formed. It also indicates that the seismic wave from the Mexico spread so fast that it reached North Dakota less than one hour.

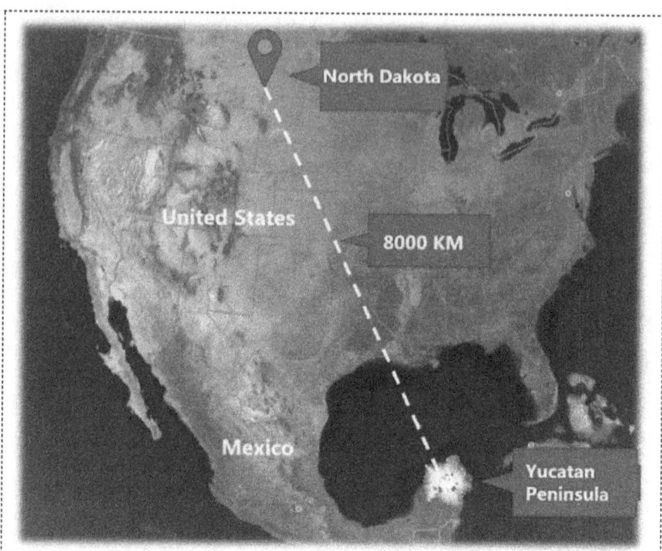

The Distance between North Dakota and Yucatan Peninsula today Has no Big Difference with the Distance at the End of Cretaceous Period

By so far, there is no evidence indicating that the Dinosaurs at the end of Cretaceous Period have the habits of living in caves and water, so, they could not counter the impact generated by the environmental changes. As terrestrial dominant animals, the large Dinosaurs face the impasse of severe food shortage all the time. Furthermore, there are growing evidences proving that the Dinosaurs are endotherms. The large endotherms need more food and energy to maintain the metabolism. So, when the K-Pg event happens, the whole food chain collapses, the large Dinosaurs that need much food are doomed to become extinct.

According to the above description, the Dinosaurs seem to become extinct in a short period after the K-Pg event. However, the scientists supporting the Asteroid Impacting

Theory believe that the extinction of the Dinosaurs is a slow process after the K-Pg event, and they discovered strong evidences for the slow extinction of the Dinosaurs.

First, the kinds and quantity of the Dinosaurs decreased at the end of Cretaceous Period. The scientists find out that the fossils of the Dinosaurs in the stratum 3 meters below the K-Pg Boundary are very few and scattered, it means that the kinds and quantity of the Dinosaurs are on the decrease. Nevertheless, the time span of Maastrichtian Stage (the last stage of Cretaceous Period) is only half of Campanian, if the kinds and quantity are divided by the time span, it can be known that the diversity of the Dinosaurs at the end of Cretaceous Period is not low. Actually, there are other factors contributing to the decrease of the kinds and quantity of the Dinosaurs, the removal of geographical separation is one factor of such kind, for instance, the disappearance of inland seaway in North America turned North America into a unified continent.

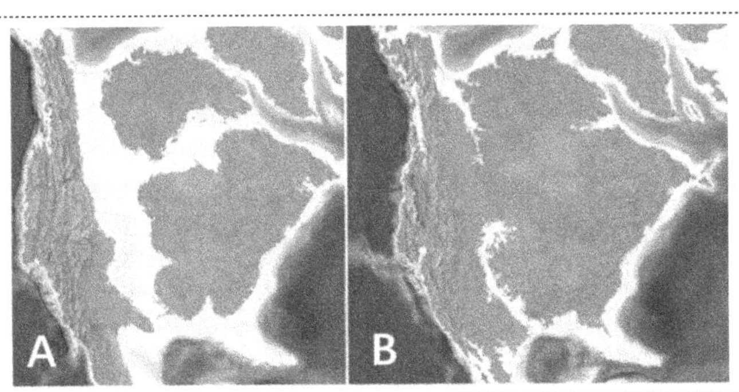

The Disappearance of Inland Seaway in North America

Figure A: End of Campanian (75 million Years Ago)

Figure B: End of Maastrichtian Stage (66 Million Years Ago)

A Great Mystery—Exploration of Dinosaurs Extinction

Second, Hadrosaur survived the K-Pg Event (5th Mass Extinction) and lived to the Paleocene Epoch. The scientists supporting the slow extinction of the Dinosaurs claim that they discovered 34 skeletal fossils of Hadrosaur, including the femur, in Ojo Alamo Sandstone of San Juan River in Utah, nearby these skeletal fossils, there are pollen samples of Palaeocene Epoch, it means that Hadrosaur survived the K-Pg Event and lived to the Palaeocene Epoch.

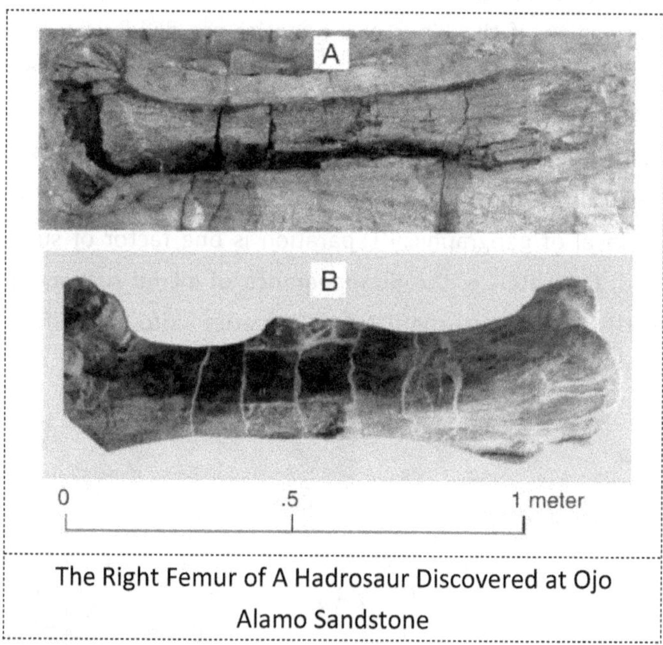

The Right Femur of A Hadrosaur Discovered at Ojo Alamo Sandstone

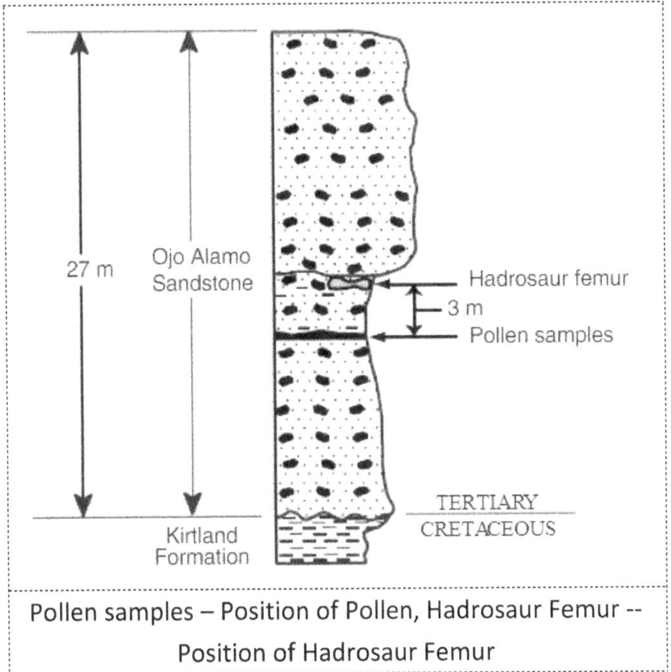

Pollen samples – Position of Pollen, Hadrosaur Femur --
Position of Hadrosaur Femur

However, as all the Dinosaur remains come from the Naashoibito Formation, the bottom of Ojo Alamo Sandstone, some scientists conclude that the Ojo Alamo Sandstone is deposited in late period of Maastrichtian Stage at the edge of Cretaceous Period. Some research fellows do not agree to such conclusion, they believe that the above Hadrosaur fossils are taken away from the original place probably due to the erosion effect, and are deposited once again in the relative young sedimentary stratum.

Third, volcanic eruptions break out in Deccan Traps. The Asteroid impacting the Earth (Yucatan Peninsula) about 65 million years ago triggered massive volcanic eruptions on Deccan Plateau in the south of India. A series of volcanic eruption lasts nearly thirty thousand years. The thickness of basalt formed by the volcanic eruptions exceeds 2000 meters. The estimated maximum area of Deccan Flood Basalts Province (a huge ocean of magma covering the area of several hundred thousand square kilometers and one thousand meters high in Indian Deccan Plateau) is 1.50 million square kilometers, equal to half of the territory of India. Owing to the erosion effect of years and continental drift, Deccan Flood Basalts Province shrank to the size today.

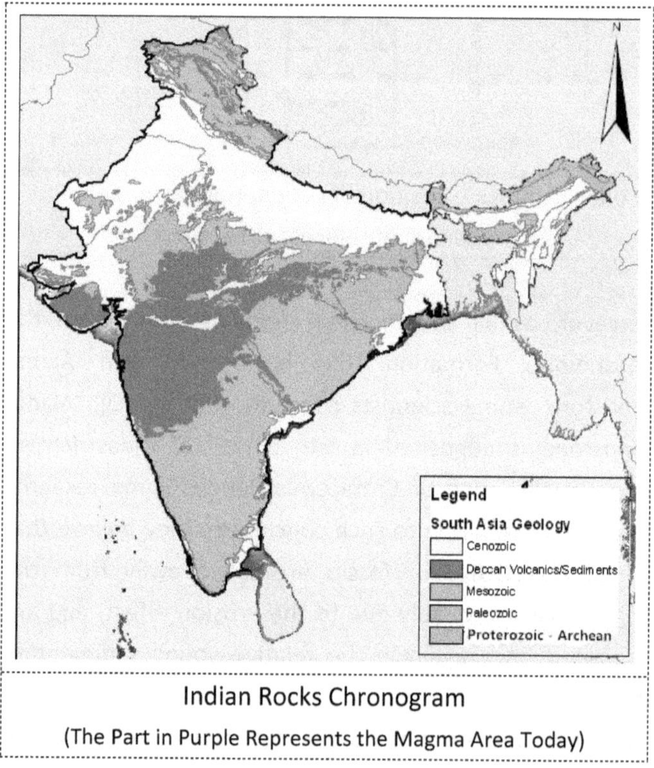

Indian Rocks Chronogram

(The Part in Purple Represents the Magma Area Today)

The gas spouted from the lasting volcanic eruptions contributes to the global warming, the plants and animals die out gradually. The evidences indicate that the

A Great Mystery—Exploration of Dinosaurs Extinction

atmosphere temperature once rose by 8℃ within 500,000 years prior to the asteroid impacting Yucatan Peninsula. Therefore, some scientists believe that the lasting volcanic eruption is the primary contributor to the extinction of the Dinosaurs, the asteroid impacting only played a role of accelerating the process of such mass extinction of the Dinosaurs rather than a critical factor.

Besides the famous and undisputable Chicxulub Crater, a few probable craters are discovered at the K-T Boundary stratum. For instance, the Boltysh Crater discovered in Ukraine, it is about 65.17 million years old and its diameter is 24 kilometers, the Silverpit Crater discovered in the North Sea, it is formed about 65~ 60 million years ago and, its diameter is 20 kilometers, and the Shiva Crater located at the open sea of India in Paleo-Tethys Ocean (*prehistoric ocean, existed from Paleozoic Era to Triassic Period, located between Hunic Terrane and Gondwanaland, equal to the Indian Ocean and South Asia today. As it is similar to the relict Mediterranean Sea between Europe and Africa today, Paleo-Tethys Ocean is also known as Tethys, the modern Mediterranean Sea is the relict waters of Tethys Sea.*), etc. So, some scientists believe that the multiple asteroids impacting the Earth contribute to the extinction of the Dinosaurs, Yucatan Impacting is no more than the last straw.

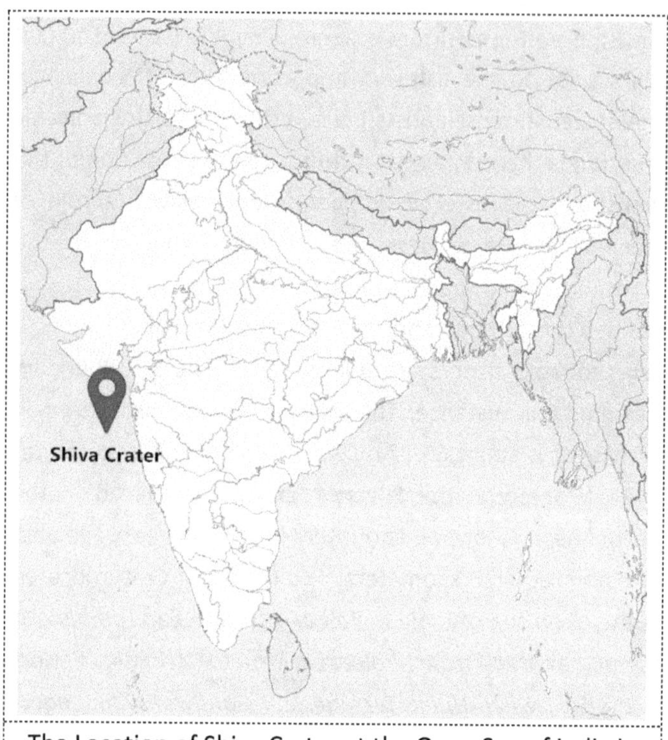

The Location of Shiva Crater at the Open Sea of India in Paleo-Tethys Ocean

However, some research findings conclude that the above craters, except for Chicxulub Crater, are the vestiges of massive volcanic activities rather than the outcome of the asteroid impacting, they are the geologic formation of stratum subsidence in essence. Except for the Chicxulub Crater, other craters are still controversial and under debate.

Owing to the support by most scientific and convincing evidences, Asteroid Impacting Theory remains the most authoritative and popular theory on the Dinosaurs extinction by so far. Notwithstanding, the Theory still has many doubts and challenged by many people. The main doubts can be summarized as follows:

(i) The mammals and some reptiles, the frogs, crocodiles and other animals living in the same era of the Dinosaurs and very sensitive to the air temperature survived the K–Pg Event, the Theory cannot explain why only the Dinosaurs became extinct; *(Arguments for the Theory or Explanation: the temperature is vital to the animals and plants. The birds, mammals, small cold-blooded reptiles, frogs, panda, crocodiles and other animals living in the same era of the Dinosaurs are small in body, need less energy, have furs to preserve body temperature, so they survived the catastrophe.)*

(ii) The Dinosaurs are the most successful animal on the Earth in Cretaceous Period, they have extensive diversities in size, shape and way of life. If the Asteroid Impacting the Earth leads to the extinction of the Dinosaurs, why the birds can survive the catastrophe and live to now?

(iii) The genera of the Dinosaurs in the stratum in the West of North America decrease gradually after the K–Pg Event, the ammonites gradually declined and perished in the later stage of Cretaceous Period. Besides, the unearthed Dinosaurs fossils indicate that the Dinosaurs died out gradually within several million years rather than within several months after the K–Pg Event. In the stratum formed after the K–Pg Event 65 million years ago, some Dinosaurs skeletons are discovered. For instance, the remains of the Dinosaurs are discovered in the stratums formed around 60 million years ago in New Mexico, and the fossils of Triceratops are discovered in the permafrost of Cenozoic Era in Alaska. The most possible reason for the gradual extinction of the Dinosaurs after the K–Pg Event is that they could not adapt to the new climate and environment.

(iv) The huge asteroid impacting the Earth in that era does not mean that it caused the mass extinction of the species, including the Dinosaurs. Many species living in the same era of the Dinosaurs survived the catastrophe. In other geologic eras, huge asteroids also impacted the Earth, but there is no abnormality in the fossils distribution of the eras. Furthermore, it is very hard to find the vestiges of the asteroid impacting the Earth left over from other mass extinctions.

(v) The latest palaeontology research findings show that the tiny tropical zone survived the catastrophe leading to the extinction of the Dinosaurs 65 million years ago. Furthermore, the argument that the asteroid impacting the Earth led to the increase of Iridium in the stratum and caused the extinction of the Dinosaurs also has some doubts:

(i) Asteroid generally comprises silicon and iron, it is impossible that no vestige is left after such huge asteroid crashed on the Earth although it experienced very long period of time, and by so far, no such huge aerolite is discovered on the Earth. *(The argument for the Theory or Explanation: The asteroid will produce huge heat when it passes through the atmosphere and crashes on the Earth and the momentum produced in colliding with the Earth is very powerful. So, the asteroid is smashed into pieces or explodes when it impacts the Earth, then it is vaporized and burned up by the huge heat.)*

(II) The most of rock stratums at the end of Cretaceous Period are the igneous rock formed by molten rock cooling, the sedimentary rock deposited by the dust only accounts for a very small portion of the Earth surface. It is impossible that the dust thrown up by an asteroid impacting the Earth can bury the most of plants and animals into the rock stratums several thousand meters thick. *(The argument for the Theory or Explanation:* the shock wave produced by the asteroid impacting will trigger or exacerbate the volcanic activity of the Earth and the volcanic ash will expand the dust produced by the asteroid impacting. The rocks several thousand meters thick are not formed within a short period, they are the formed after long-period deposit and are not produced in the mass extinction, they are the rock stratums produced in the long-period natural evolution during the whole Cretaceous Period and cannot be used as the reference to the mass extinction.)

(iii) Can the Iridium contained in an asteroid distribute evenly and spread around the Earth? The Iridium also exists deep inside the Earth and it will be spouted to the Earth surface by the volcanic activity. So, it cannot be concluded that the Iridium comes from the outer space. *(Arguments for the Theory or Explanation: the asteroid will explode and burn up when it impacts the Earth, the Iridium enters into the atmosphere and spread around the Earth with air circulation. Actually the Iridium is not distributed evenly on the Earth, the Iridium content in some places is high while low in other places. The Chicxulub Crater, shocked quartz, squashed sand and graveyard in North Dakota fully testify the conclusion that a huge asteroid impacted the Earth 65 million years ago. The Iridium content in the K-T Boundary is consistent with the Iridium content in the asteroid, it can be ascertained that the Iridium on the Earth principally comes from the asteroid, the Iridium coming from the core of the Earth in the volcanic activity is only very small portion. The might of the volcanic activity, including the volcanic activity in Deccan Traps, is far less than the might of the Yucatan impacting event, the might of the volcanic activity is far from being adequate for causing such severe mass extinction of species.*)

(iv) There are five concentrations of Iridium in the K-T Boundary in Italy, it is impossible that the huge asteroid will impact the Earth for consecutive five times.

So, the asteroid impacting the Earth is not the decisive factor contributing to the extinction of the Dinosaurs, it may play a role of accelerating the extinction of the Dinosaurs.

A number of scientists insist that the frequent volcanic activity, climate change or emerging of mammals are the primary contributors to the extinction of the Dinosaurs.

Due to the above doubts and challenges, the Asteroid Impacting Theory is not accepted universally as the final conclusion or right answer on the extinction of the Dinosaurs although it remains the most authoritative and popular theory on this issue by so far. Probably nothing is final or absolutely right in this world.

IV.   New Exploration -- Most Possible and Reasonable Cause of Dinosaurs Extinction

The facts and general knowledge reveals that the natural environment is the primary factor deciding the forms of life being. The natural environment is a system that comprises the climate, atmosphere composition, temperature, ecosystem, water, soil, continents, oceans, mountains, rivers and other relevant elements. Each species needs a proper environment for normal growth, the emerging or extinction of a species is closely associated with natural environment in which it lives. The change of natural environment can promote the emerging of some species and cause the decline and extinction of other species. In the Dinosaurs era, there is no man-made pollution and human activities disturbing the natural environment, the change of natural environment can only be attributed to the inside and outside factors. The inside factors come from the movement and evolution of the Earth itself and the outside factors come from the movement and evolution of Solar System.

Except for the Asteroid Impacting Theory, the other theories put forward by the scientists by so far on the extinction of the Dinosaurs are specious because the arguments and scenario of these theories are based on the seemingly logical speculation and imagination rather than demonstration, for instance, the Climate Change Theory does not specify what causes the climate change, the Crust Movement Theory does not tell what causes the crust movement. Even the Asteroid Impacting Theory, its scenario after the asteroid impacting the Earth is also based on computer modeling and speculation. Nevertheless, most of these theories, including the Asteroid Impacting Theory, are common in one point, namely one or more inside factors and/or outside factors lead to the change of natural environment proper for the survival of the Dinosaurs, such as catastrophe, climate change, dramatic drop or sudden rise of temperature, cooling, atmosphere composition change, seal level receding, acid rain, ecosystem damage, drought, massive death of plants and emerging of new species, etc., the Dinosaurs could not adapt to such change, or change themselves to suit the new environment, so they became extinct. However, such common point still has defect or doubt, namely the effect of inside or outside factor(s) on the Earth natural environment is short and limited, it may change the natural environment for a short period rather than permanently. The natural environment will restore to the original or normal state after the effect on the Earth natural environment weakens or disappears, provided that the Earth continues to revolve around the Sun and the distance between the Sun and Earth remains unchanged. The remaining species surviving the extinction or catastrophe, including the Dinosaurs, could continue to exist and live as normal. So, the question comes up, what are the ultimate factors deciding the form of the Earth natural environment? The answer is: the Sun and the distance between the Earth and Sun. The Sun gives the Earth and other planets of the Solar System the light and heat. The temperature is vital to the origin and evolution of life and is the measurement of light and heat. In the

Solar System, the temperature levels of the plants, including the Earth, are dependent on the intensity or strength of the light and heat received from the Sun, the intensity or strength of the light and heat received by the planets is dependent on the distance away from the Sun. The Venus is too close to the Sun, its temperature is too high, exceeding 400℃, the water exists in gaseous state, the Mars is too far away from the Sun, its temperature is too low, lower than -100℃, the water exists in solid state. These two neighbor planets of the Earth have no life or are "dead" as they are too hot and too cold and not appropriate for the origin and evolution of life. The Earth has life or is "live", it testifies that the distance between the Sun and the Earth is the distance proper for the origin and evolution of life. Compared with the Venus and the Mars, the Earth is neither too close to nor too far away from the Sun, the intensity or strength of the light and heat received from the Sun contributes to a moderate temperature that makes water exist in the water can exist in in gaseous, liquid and solid states. So, the Sun and the distance between the Sun and the Earth jointly decide the form of Earth natural environment right for the origin and evolution of life, or put it in another way, the distance between the Sun and the Earth is the distance for life. Suppose one day the Earth is pushed by an outside super-powerful force to the position or orbit of the Venus or the Mars, it is no doubt that life will vanish and no longer exist. If the Earth is pushed by an outside force to   a new position more close to or farther away from the Sun (not the position of the Venus or the Mars), deviating its original orbit a little, the Earth natural environment will be changed accordingly and dramatically, the species that could not adept to new environment will become extinct and new species will emerge in the new natural environment.

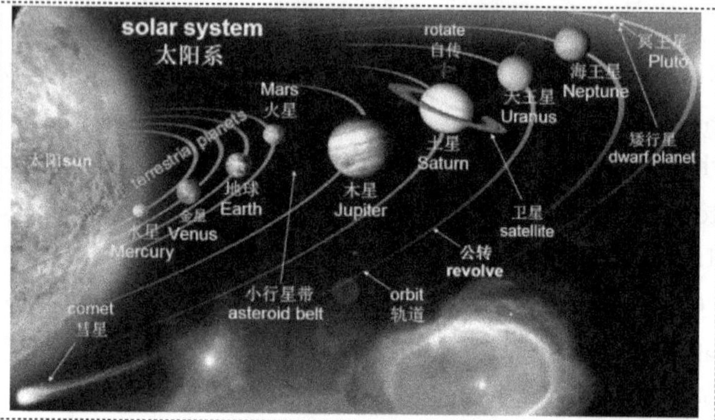

The Solar System Comprising Nine Planets Revolving Around the Sun

The Earth --- Only One Planet That Has Life in the Solar System

A Great Mystery—Exploration of Dinosaurs Extinction

Based on the above analysis, the most possible and reasonable cause of the Dinosaurs extinction comes to the surface, that is, the extinction of a species can be attributed to one or more causes that lead to the universal, irreversible, unrecoverable or permanent change of the natural environment on which the species is dependent. As the species could not adapt to the new changes, it became extinct. Looking at the heavy height and huge body of the large Dinosaurs (the Dinosaurs are reptiles, they are numerous and diverse in variety and different in shape, the large Dinosaurs weigh 40~50 tons and even to 100 tons and are several dozens of meters long in body length, the small Dinosaurs are less than one meter in body length.), it can be inferred that the Earth gravity and atmosphere pressure in the Dinosaurs Era are far smaller than the same today and the geographic and climate conditions are relatively stable and remain unchanged for a long period of time (at least 160 million years as the Dominated the global terrestrial ecosystem for 160 million years.). As the Earth gravity is very small, many mountain peaks are steep and very high, but do not collapse, the trees can grow as high as several dozens of meters, but do not topple due to their own weight, and in the same way, the large Dinosaurs weighing several dozens of tons to one hundred tons are not crushed by their own heavy weight, furthermore, they can walks and run lightly on the Earth. The Earth gravity is so small that the small Dinosaurs could jump longer distance so long as they grasp the skills and wield the four legs properly. In the natural environment with so small Earth gravity, the small Dinosaurs gradually evolve into the flying Dinosaurs and finally evolve into the birds today. So, it is fair to say that the flying Dinosaurs are the ancestors of the birds today, and the birds today are the living fossils of the Dinosaurs.

The Dinosaurs of Different Shapes and Sizes

It can be imagined that it is impossible for a terrestrial animal to evolve into a flying one if it had not been for a very small Earth gravity in that era. Under the Earth gravity today, such feeling can only be found under microgravity or buoyancy of water. Till one day, a huge asteroid impacted the Earth, the super-powerful energy triggered the unprecedented violent earthquake, the high mountain peaks collapsed under drastic jounce and trembling, the plants on the slopes slid down to the valley bottom first, then they are buried together by the subsequent slumped soils and sandstones, forming the later large-scale coal bed. Meanwhile, some Dinosaurs could not escape such catastrophe from the universe and were buried along with the plants in the valley bottom in the rush for survival, which can explain why the Dinosaur fossils of different kinds are discovered in the same one place.

The smoke dust and earthquake produced by the asteroid impacting the Earth are far from powerful enough to kill off most of the Dinosaurs as the Dinosaurs are distributed globally and are diverse in variety. The true cause leading to the extinction of the Dinosaurs is that the huge impact force of the asteroid drove the Earth deviate from the original orbit revolving around the Sun, or changed the rotation velocity of the Earth, thereby the Earth gravity and atmosphere pressure are changed, leading to the fundamental, universal, irreversible, unrecoverable or permanent change of the Earth natural environment. After asteroid impacting the Earth and the consequent earthquakes, the Earth gravity increased, the weight of the Dinosaurs rose consequently, the majority of large Dinosaurs could no longer stand up or walk as their original muscles and skeleton are no longer strong enough to support their weight under the increased Earth gravity, they have no way out in the new natural environment. Similarly, some small Dinosaurs could no longer stand up after their weight increased suddenly, but luckily their weight is relatively light compared with the large Dinosaurs, they can walk and survive barely by dropping their abdomen down on the ground to support their body, gradually they evolved into the crocodiles, tortoises, lizards, snakes and other reptiles today in the new natural environment. These reptiles are the living fossils of the Dinosaurs era. If the four legs of a crocodile are rectified to enable it to stand up, it can be seen that the crocodile is actually a small Dinosaur.

Some Dinosaurs living nearby the lakes, rivers or coast survived the new natural environment by sheltering themselves in the water to support their body with aid of the buoyancy of water when the Earth gravity increased, but they could no longer go ashore and only can live in the water, gradually they evolved into the whales, walrus, Phoca vitulina (harbor seal) and other aquatic mammals.

The Dinosaurs surviving the catastrophe (most of them are small Dinosaurs), the primitive birds (Proavis) and the mammals evolved from the Dinosaurs in Jurassic period, under the rule of "Survival of the Fittest in Natural Selection" and in the new natural environment, changed their original shapes after continuous evolution of 70 million years, they evolved from cold-blooded animals into the warm-blooded animals capable of regulating their body temperatures (the birds, mammals and human). After a massive species evolution, some species still reserve their original shapes, for instance, after the fishes evolved into amphibians, the fishes continue to exist, and a few of the reptiles, such as the crocodiles and lizards, etc., still remains the primitive shapes of the Dinosaurs 70 million years ago.

Another most possible cause of the Dinosaurs extinction is that the Solar System and Earth in the Dinosaurs era are growing or expanding and under fast evolution in the Dinosaurs era, the asteroids collide with the Earth from time to time, thereby the mass of the Earth is on the increase, the Earth gravity and the gravity between the Sun and the Earth are rising, the Earth orbit revolving around the Sun is not stable, the Earth is deviating its orbit slowly all the time, consequently the Earth natural environment is under gradual yet constant and irreversible change. Till one day 65 million years ago, a huge asteroid impacted the Yucatan Peninsula. The impact force of the asteroid is so powerful that it pushed the Earth to a new orbit more close to the Sun, the Earth gravity and atmosphere pressure increased, directly leading to the great, universal and permanent change of the Earth natural environment. As the large Dinosaurs could not adapt to the new natural environment and became extinct in the end, the relatively small Dinosaurs evolved into the reptiles and aquatic mammals.

As the Earth is under continuous evolution, the Earth natural environment remains at the threshold state all the time, the accidental outside force may trigger the profound and irreversible change of the Earth natural environment, so the Dinosaurs are doomed to become extinct sooner or later. The asteroid impacting the Yucatan Peninsula 65 million years ago is just a last straw or the final ball leading to such outcome.

V. Conclusion and Revelation

The end of the Dinosaurs era testifies the rule of "Survival of the Fittest in Natural Selection" put forward by Charles Darwin and it also reveals the natural law that any species will inevitably experience the emergence, development, flourishing and death, just like the life experience of human. It is the natural law that cannot be changed by any force. The extinction of the Dinosaurs is the natural and normal deduction of life logics on the Earth.

The natural environment decides the forms of life. After the end of the Dinosaurs era, the Earth entered into the Cenozoic Era, the new natural environment creates the conditions for the emergence and evolution of more senior species, including human.

Everything is under constant change and continuous evolution, including the Sun, solar System and the universe. Maybe everything is at a threshold state, any outside force or accidental event could trigger great and profound changes of the world.

The Sun is the mother star and center of the Solar System, its mass accounts for 99.86% of the mass of the whole Solar System and its volume is approximately 1.30 million times the volume of the Earth. The primary chemical compositions of the Sun comprise hydrogen (71%), helium (26%) and a few relatively heavy elements, including oxygen, carbon, neon and ferrum, etc. As the Sun has extra-huge mass and volume, the pressure, density and temperature in its core zone are extremely high, triggering the huge thermonuclear reaction (Nuclear Fusion) in its core zone, thus burning the whole Sun and emitting the light and heat to its planets. Furthermore, owing to its extra huge mass, the Sun has powerful gravity to capture nine planets and drive these planets revolve around it along with its rotation. The planet most close to the Sun is the Mercury, the planet farthest away from the Sun is the Pluto, the Earth is the third planet away from the Sun. The moderate light and heat received by the Earth at its proper position from the Sun breed the life on the Earth. The asteroid belt is located between the Mars and the Jupiter and it is quite close to the Earth. So, it is inevitable and natural thing that the asteroid impacts the Earth accidently or from time to time.

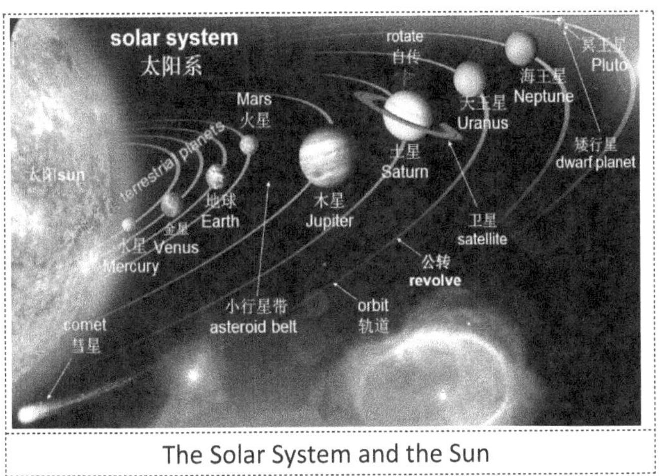

The Solar System and the Sun

The Sun is just an ordinary star in the Milky Way Galaxy, it is a burning globe and its life span is about 10 billion years, the present age of the Sun is 4.57 billion years old, it means that the Sun will be burned up 5~6 billion years later. In the course of burning, the Sun is losing its mass and its gravity to the planets is on the decrease consequently. With the decrease of the gravity of the Sun to its planets, the Pluto, the planet farthest away from the Sun, will be the first one to detach from its orbit revolving around the Sun and escape the Solar System, the next one is the Neptune, and by analogy, the Earth will gradually move to the orbit of the Mars. In this process, the Earth will be cooling slowly, its natural environment will be changed thoroughly and the life on the Earth will perish in the end.

In the broad sense, all the planets of the Sun will escape the Solar System when the gravity of the Sun is no longer powerful enough to capture them, they will become the asteroids or the planets of another Sun-like star in the Milky Way Galaxy, the same or similar story of Earth life will happen again if one of these planets enjoys the same conditions as the Earth has now. In this connection, everything, including the life, is no more than a cycle between the emergence and extinction.

---The End--